GRAPHIC SCIENCE

D1536546

THE *SURPRISING* WORLD OF BACTERIA

with MAX AXIOM SUPER SCIENTIST

4D An Augmented Reading Science Experience

by Agnieszka Biskup | illustrated by Tod G. Smith

Consultant:
Dr. Beth Traxler
Associate Professor of Microbiology
University of Washington
Seattle, Washington

CAPSTONE PRESS
a capstone imprint

Graphic Library is published by Capstone Press.
1710 Roe Crest Drive, North Mankato, Minnesota 56003.
www.capstonepub.com

Library of Congress Cataloging-in-Publication Data is available on the Library of Congress website.

ISBN: 978-1-5435-7249-0 (library binding)
ISBN: 978-1-5435-7546-0 (paperback)
ISBN: 978-1-5435-7253-7 (eBook PDF)

Summary: In graphic novel format, follows the adventures of Max Axiom
as he explains the science behind bacteria.

Designer
Alison Thiele

Colorist
Matt Webb

Production Specialist
Laura Manthe

Cover Colorist
Krista Ward

Media Researcher
Wanda Winch

Editor
Anthony Wacholtz

Photo Credits
Capstone Studio: Karon Dubke, 29, back cover;
Shutterstock: Ginaalu, 19, Sebastian Kaulitzki, 9

All internet sites appearing in back matter were available and accurate
when this book was sent to press.

1 Ask an adult to download the app.

 Capstone 4D
Education

2 Scan any page with the star.

3 Enjoy your cool stuff!

—— OR ——

Use this password at capstone4D.com

bacteria.72490

Printed in the United States of America.
PA70

TABLE OF CONTENTS

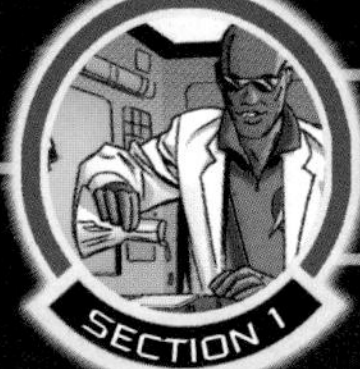
SECTION 1

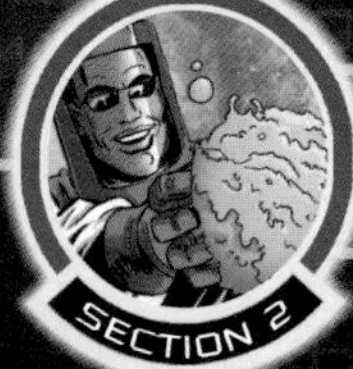
SECTION 2

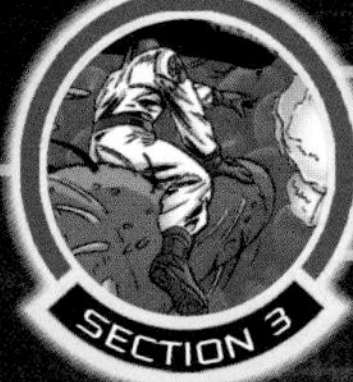
SECTION 3

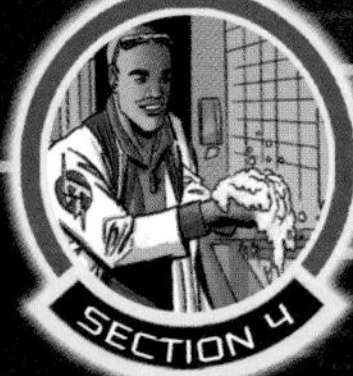
SECTION 4

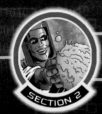

SECTION 1 IT'S A SMALL WORLD

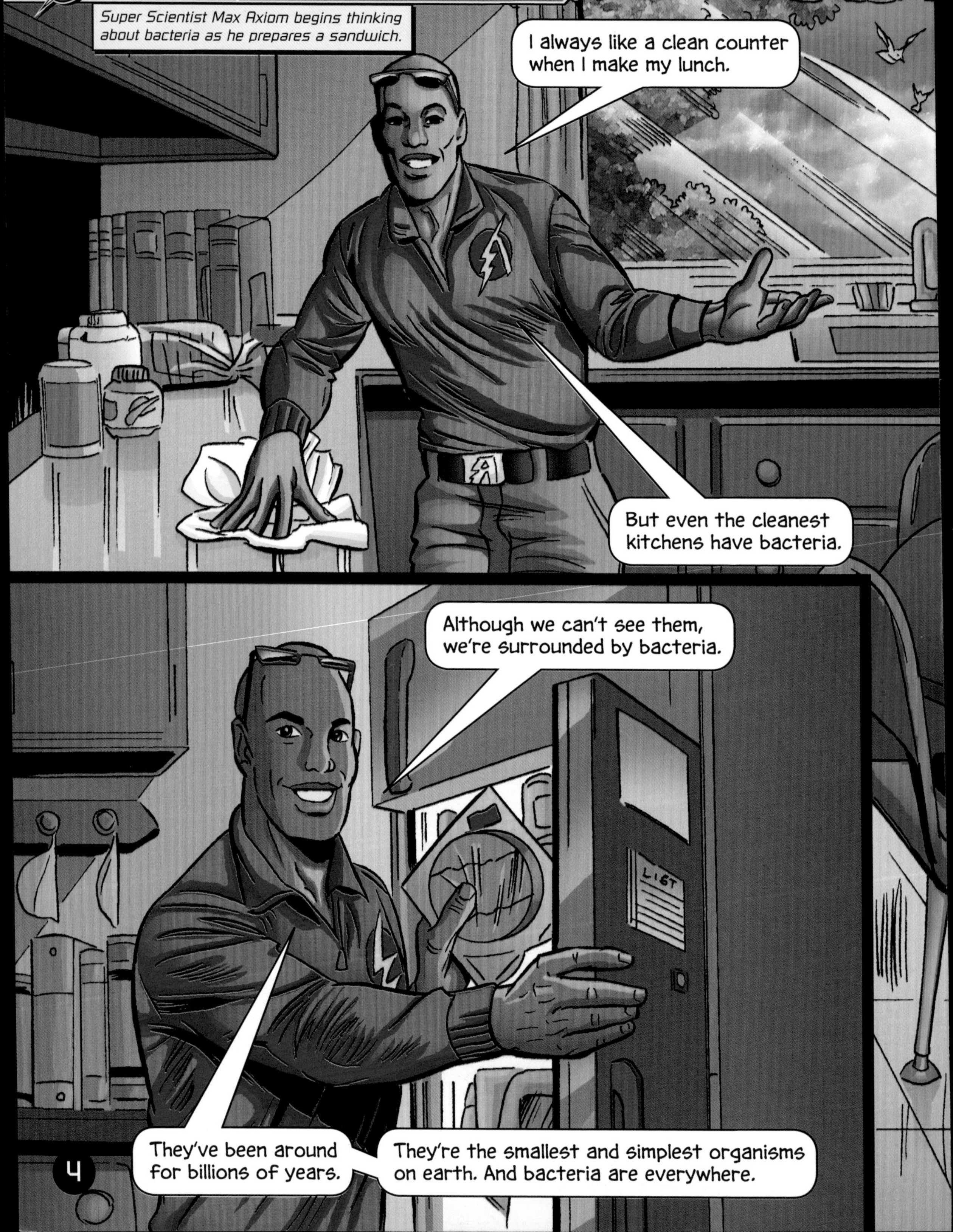
Super Scientist Max Axiom begins thinking about bacteria as he prepares a sandwich.
I always like a clean counter when I make my lunch.
But even the cleanest kitchens have bacteria.
Although we can't see them, we're surrounded by bacteria.
LIST
They've been around for billions of years.
They're the smallest and simplest organisms on earth. And bacteria are everywhere.

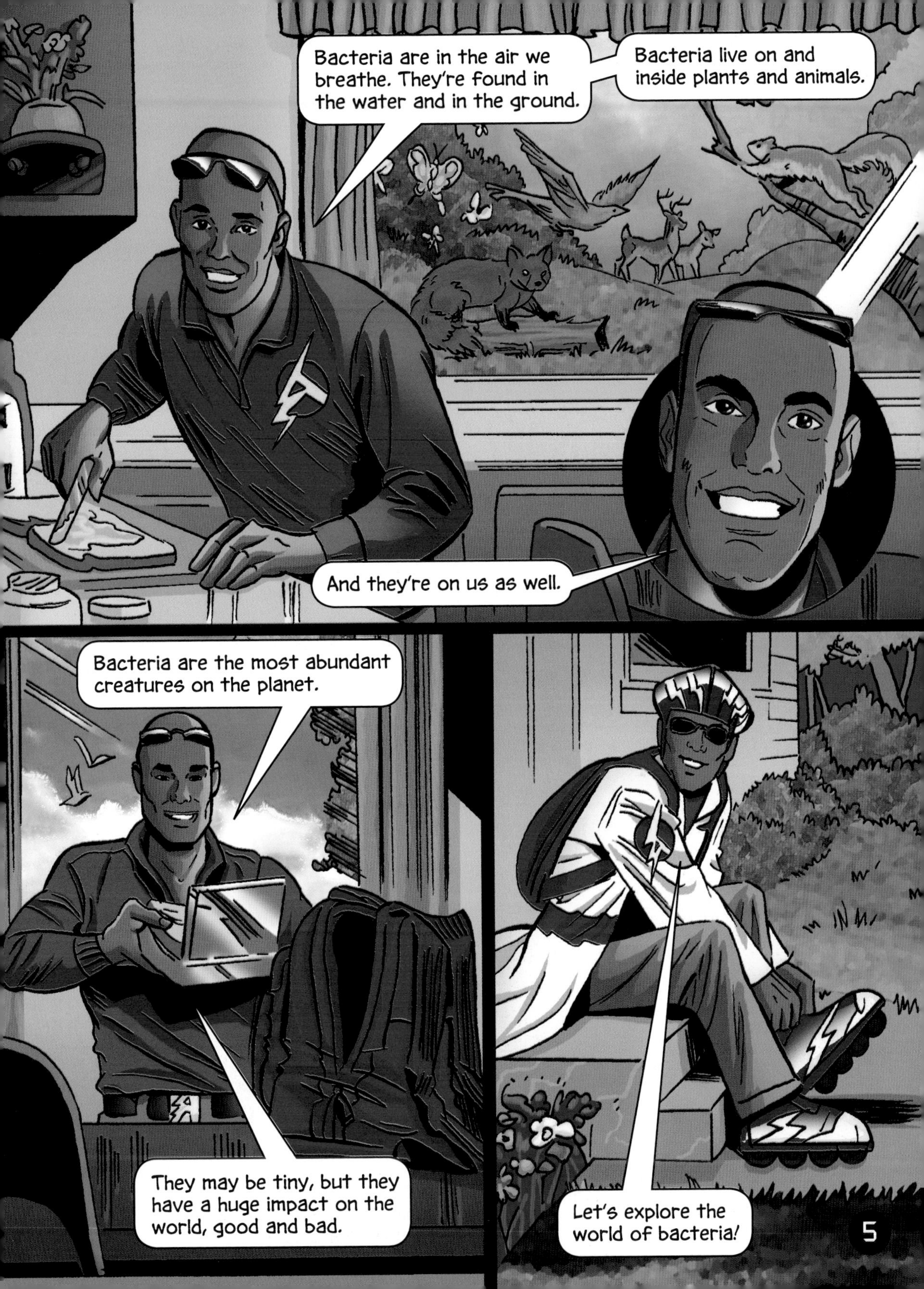
Bacteria are in the air we breathe. They're found in the water and in the ground.
Bacteria live on and inside plants and animals.
And they're on us as well.
Bacteria are the most abundant creatures on the planet.
They may be tiny, but they have a huge impact on the world, good and bad.
Let's explore the world of bacteria!

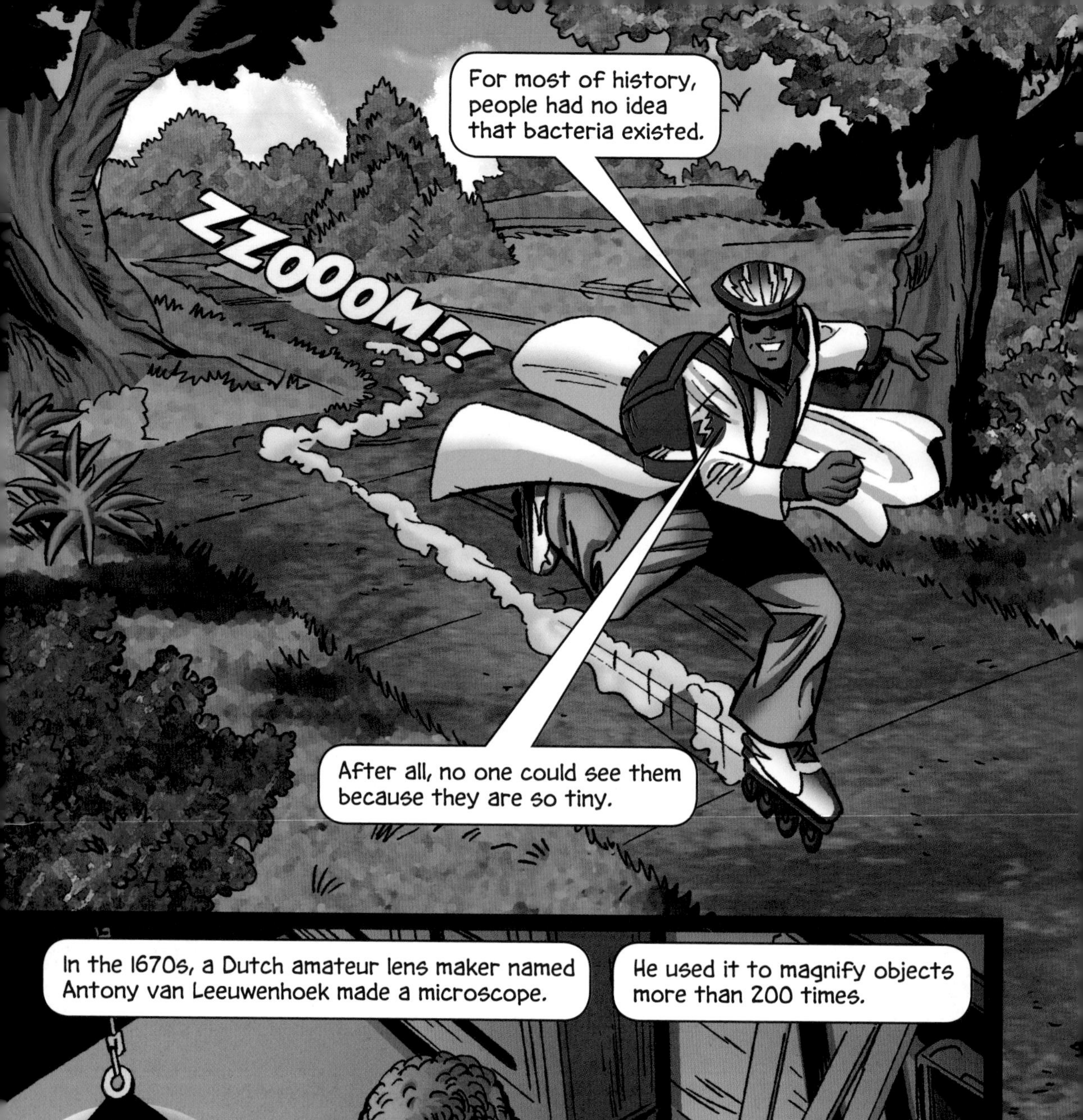
For most of history, people had no idea that bacteria existed.
ZZOOOM!!
After all, no one could see them because they are so tiny.

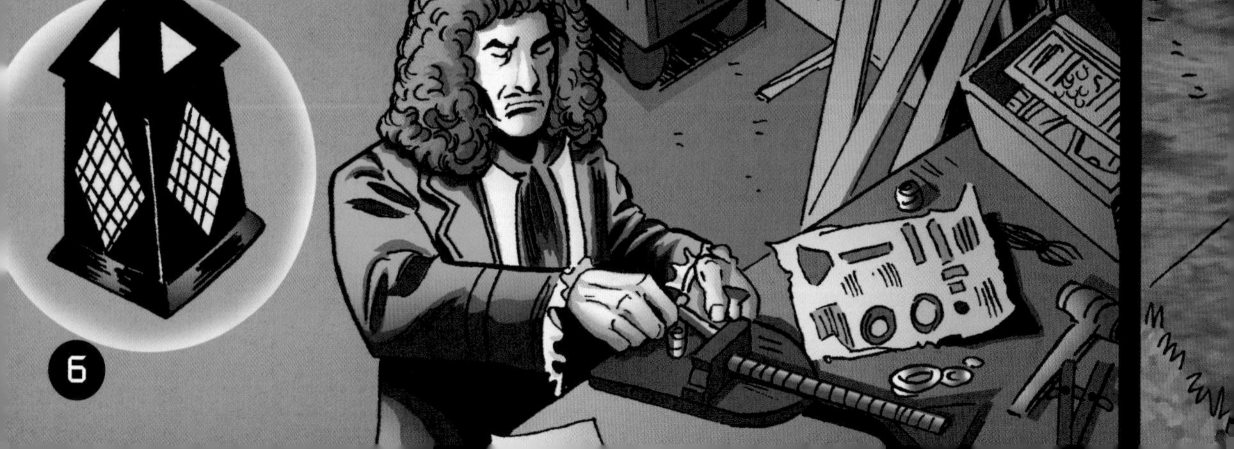
In the 1670s, a Dutch amateur lens maker named Antony van Leeuwenhoek made a microscope.
He used it to magnify objects more than 200 times.

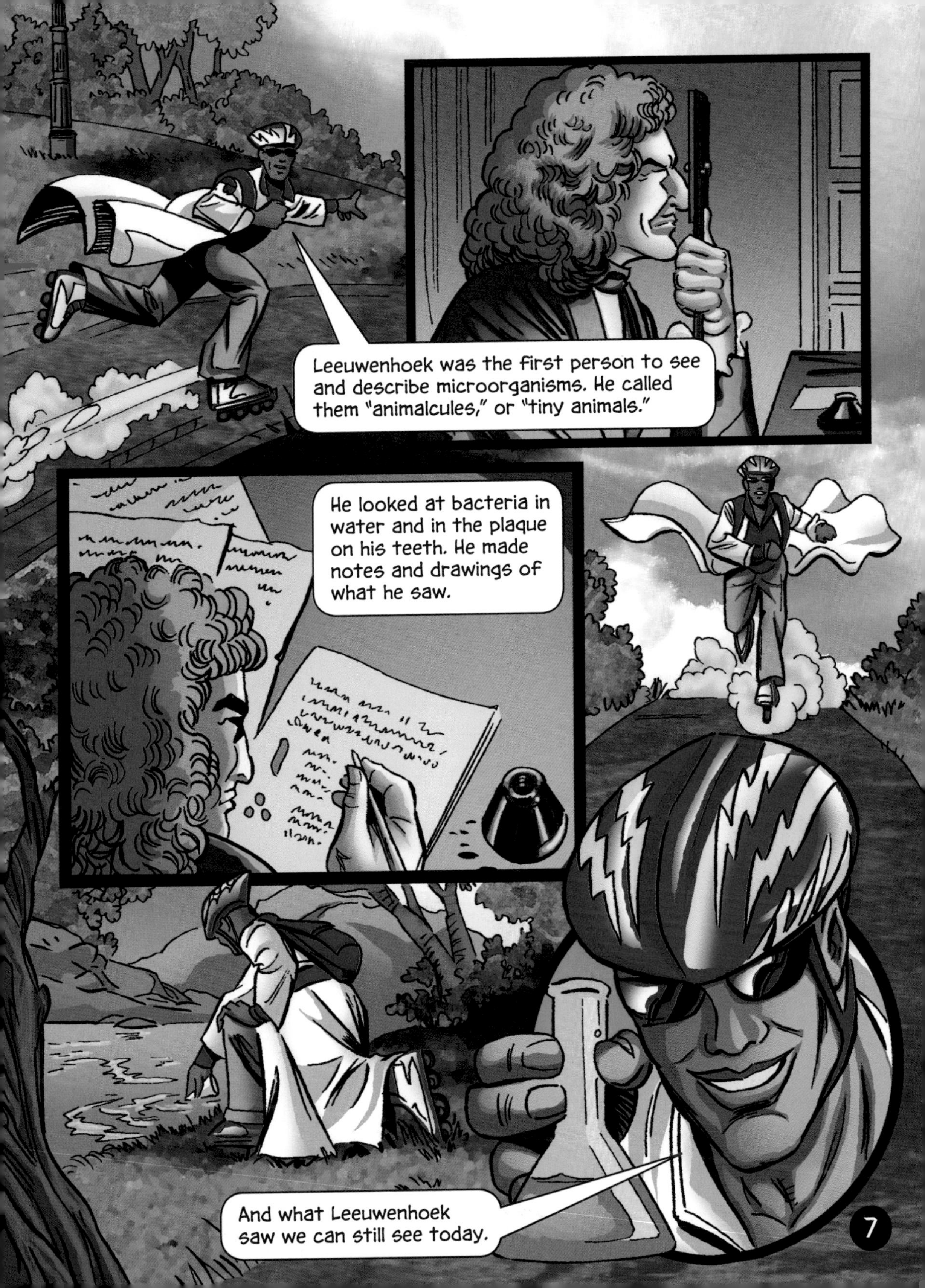
Leeuwenhoek was the first person to see and describe microorganisms. He called them "animalcules," or "tiny animals."
He looked at bacteria in water and in the plaque on his teeth. He made notes and drawings of what he saw.
And what Leeuwenhoek saw we can still see today.

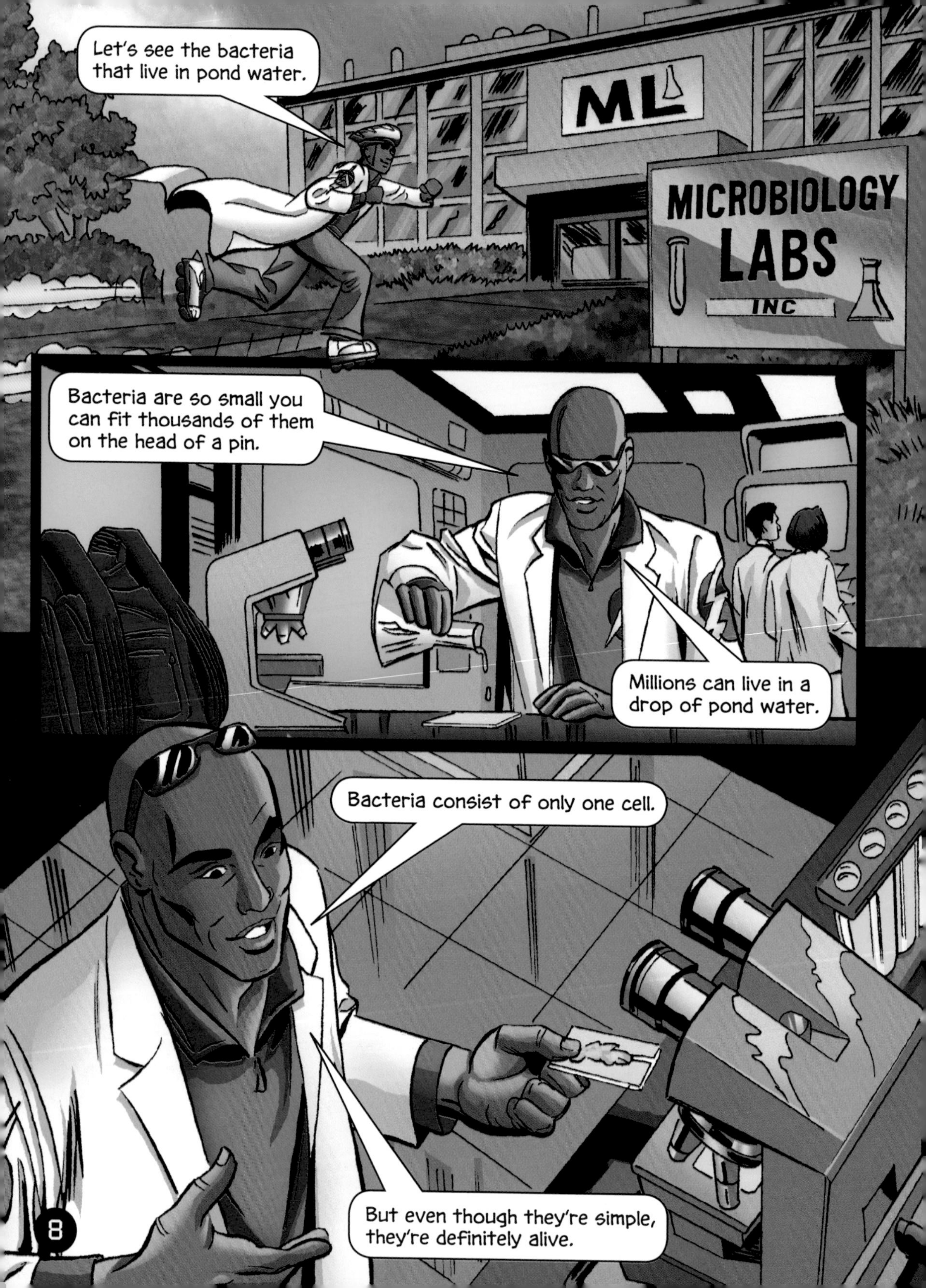
Let's see the bacteria that live in pond water.
ML
MICROBIOLOGY LABS INC
Bacteria are so small you can fit thousands of them on the head of a pin.
Millions can live in a drop of pond water.
Bacteria consist of only one cell.
But even though they're simple, they're definitely alive.

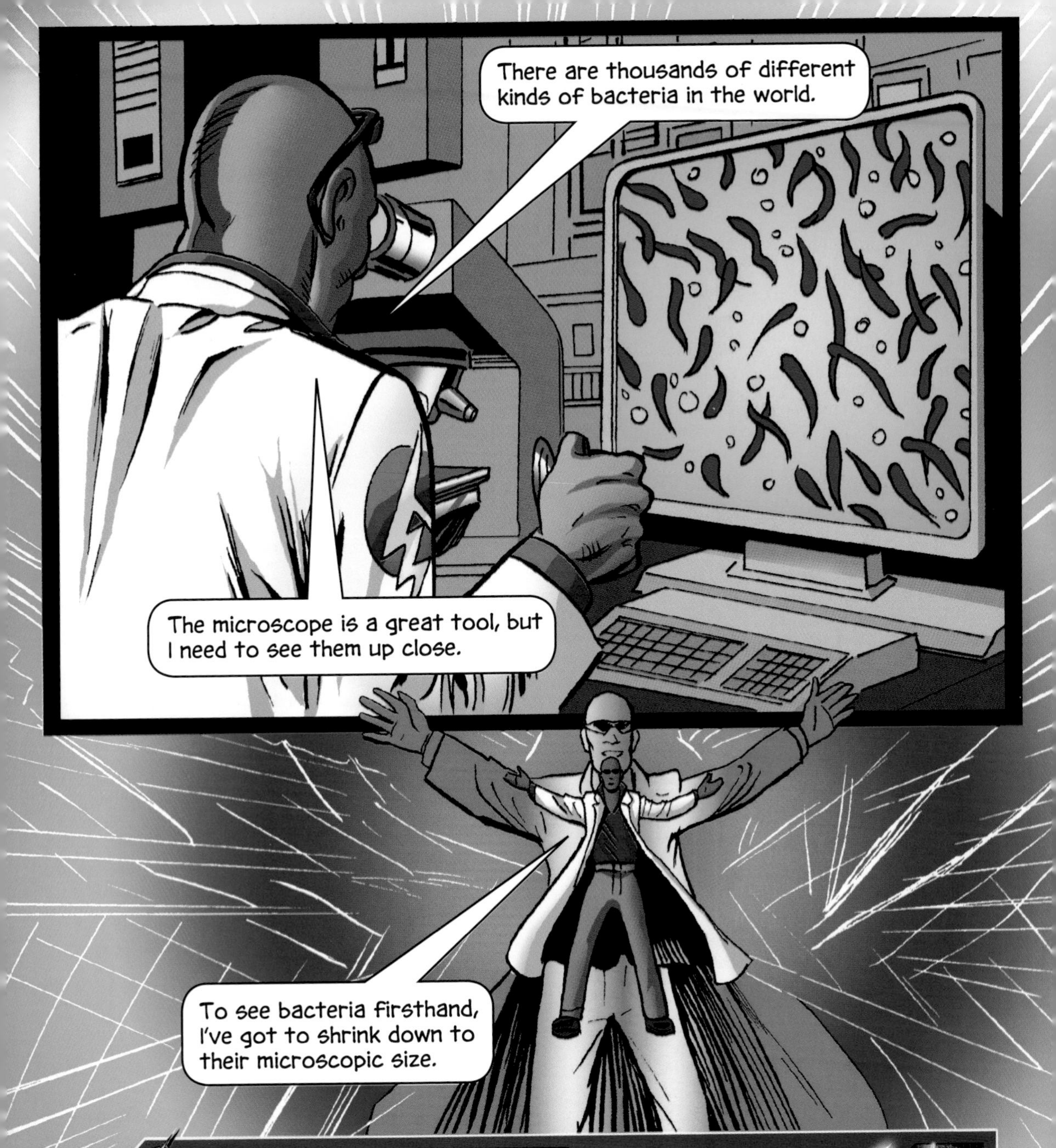
There are thousands of different kinds of bacteria in the world.
The microscope is a great tool, but I need to see them up close.
To see bacteria firsthand, I've got to shrink down to their microscopic size.

CELLS EVERYWHERE

ACCESS GRANTED: MAX AXIOM

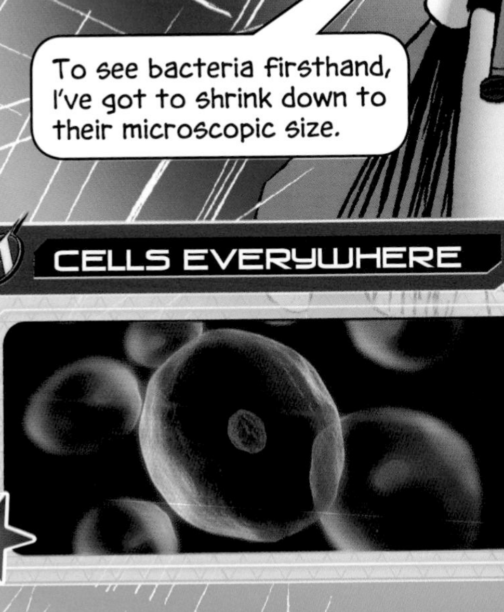

Cells are the basic unit of all living things. Every living thing is made up of one or more cells. Unlike bacteria, our bodies are made up of trillions of cells.

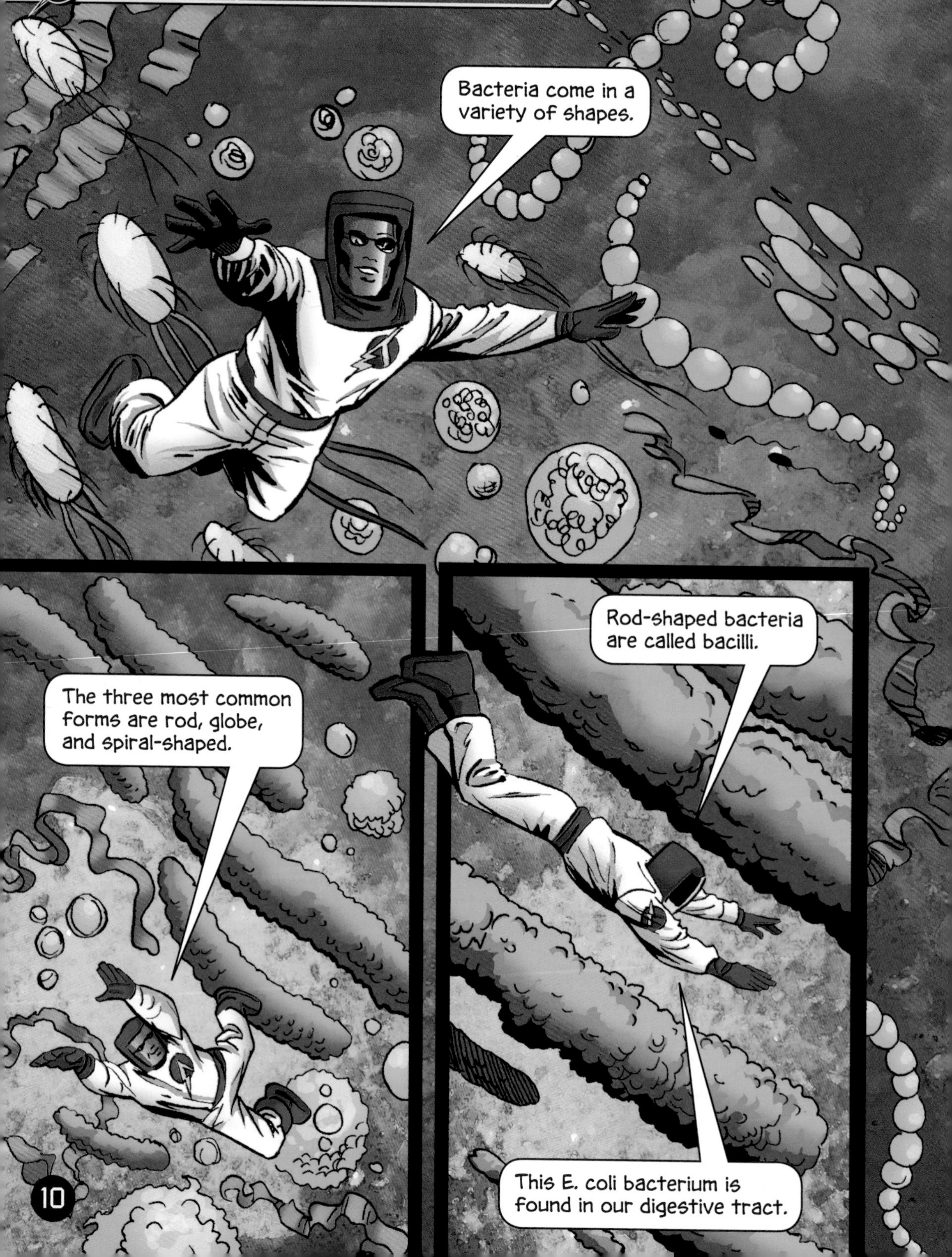
Bacteria come in a variety of shapes.
The three most common forms are rod, globe, and spiral-shaped.
Rod-shaped bacteria are called bacilli.
This E. coli bacterium is found in our digestive tract.

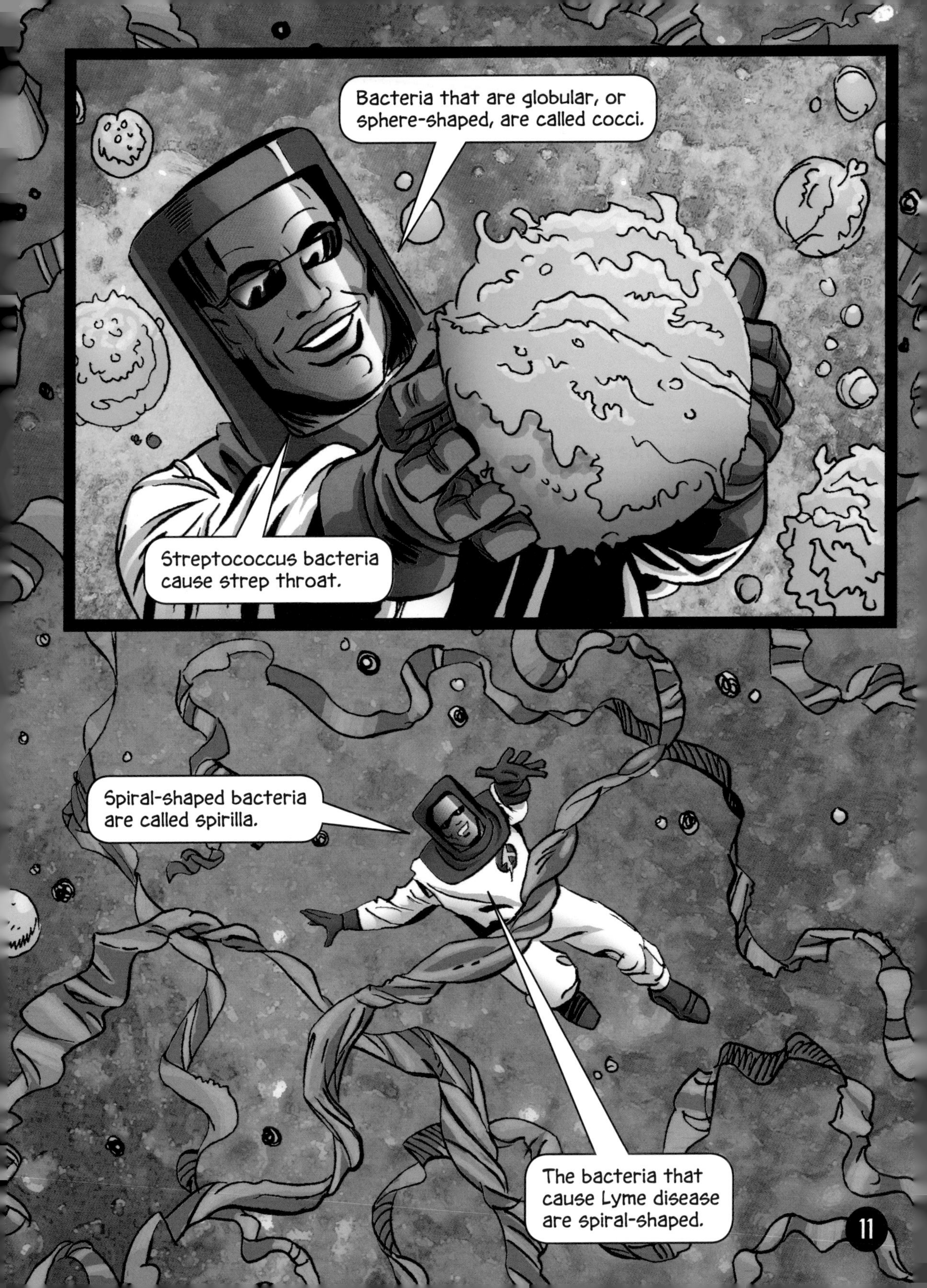

Bacteria that are globular, or sphere-shaped, are called cocci.
Streptococcus bacteria cause strep throat.
Spiral-shaped bacteria are called spirilla.
The bacteria that cause Lyme disease are spiral-shaped.

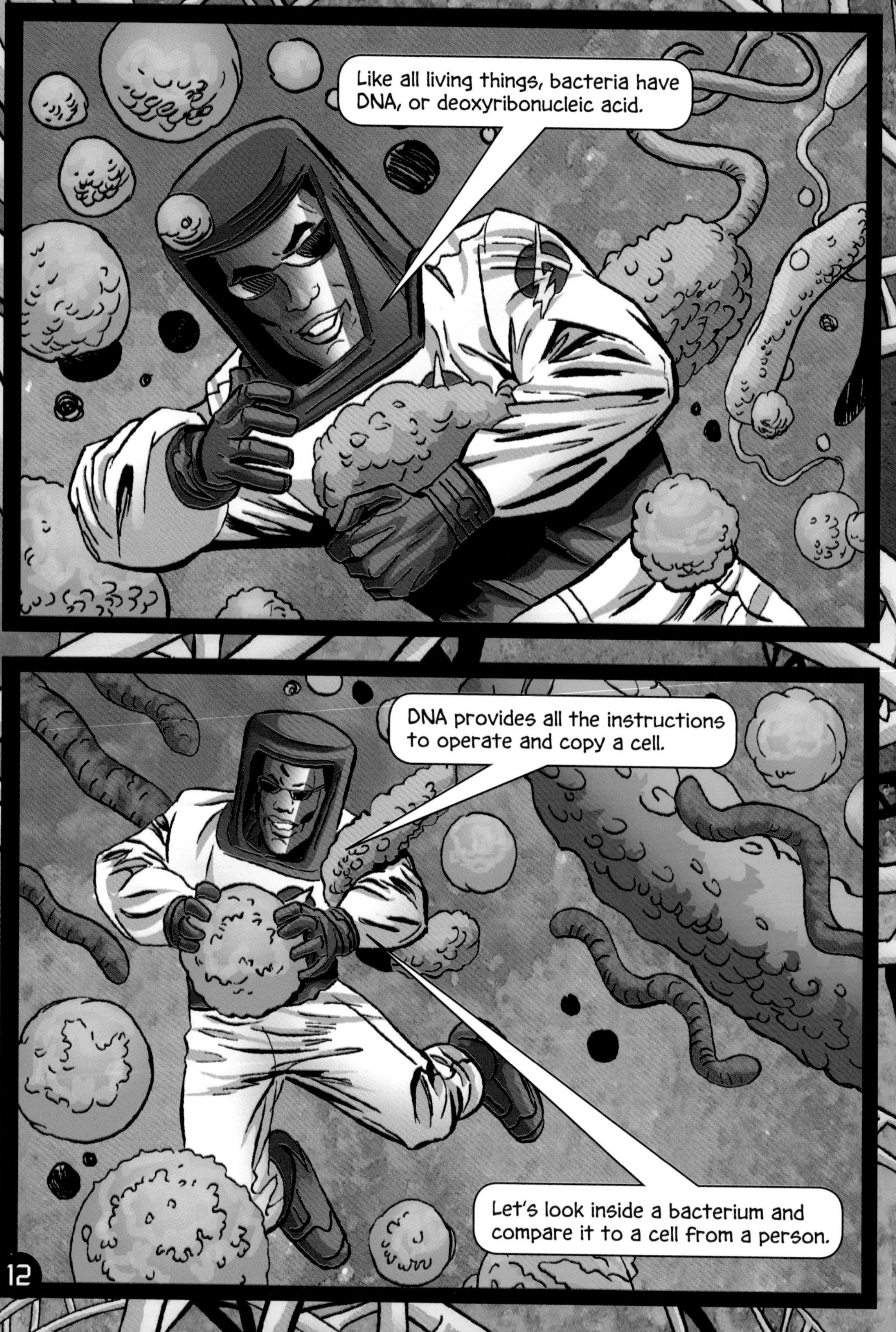
Like all living things, bacteria have DNA, or deoxyribonucleic acid.
DNA provides all the instructions to operate and copy a cell.
Let's look inside a bacterium and compare it to a cell from a person.

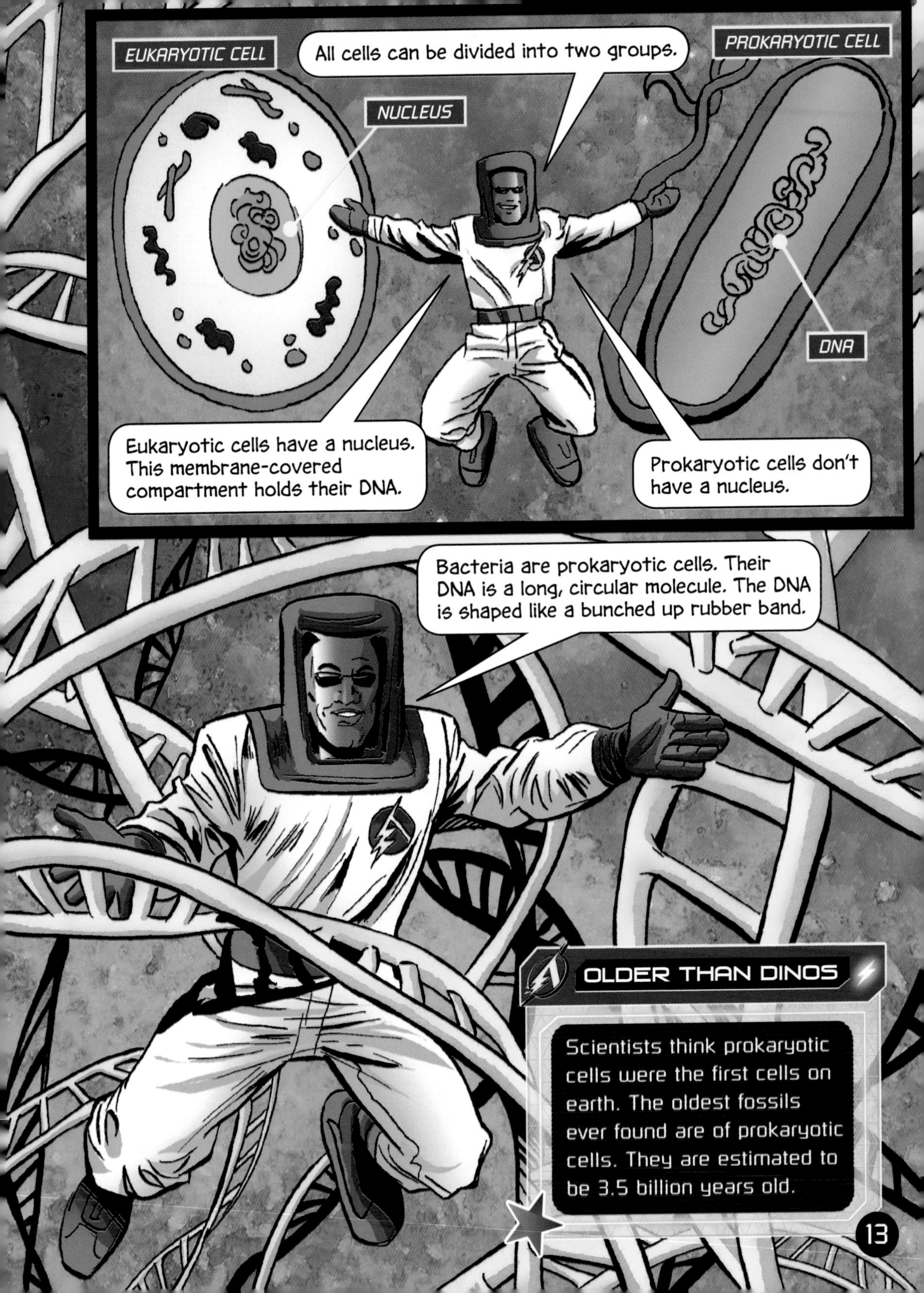
EUKARYOTIC CELL
All cells can be divided into two groups.
PROKARYOTIC CELL
NUCLEUS
DNA
Eukaryotic cells have a nucleus. This membrane-covered compartment holds their DNA.
Prokaryotic cells don't have a nucleus.
Bacteria are prokaryotic cells. Their DNA is a long, circular molecule. The DNA is shaped like a bunched up rubber band.
OLDER THAN DINOS
Scientists think prokaryotic cells were the first cells on earth. The oldest fossils ever found are of prokaryotic cells. They are estimated to be 3.5 billion years old.

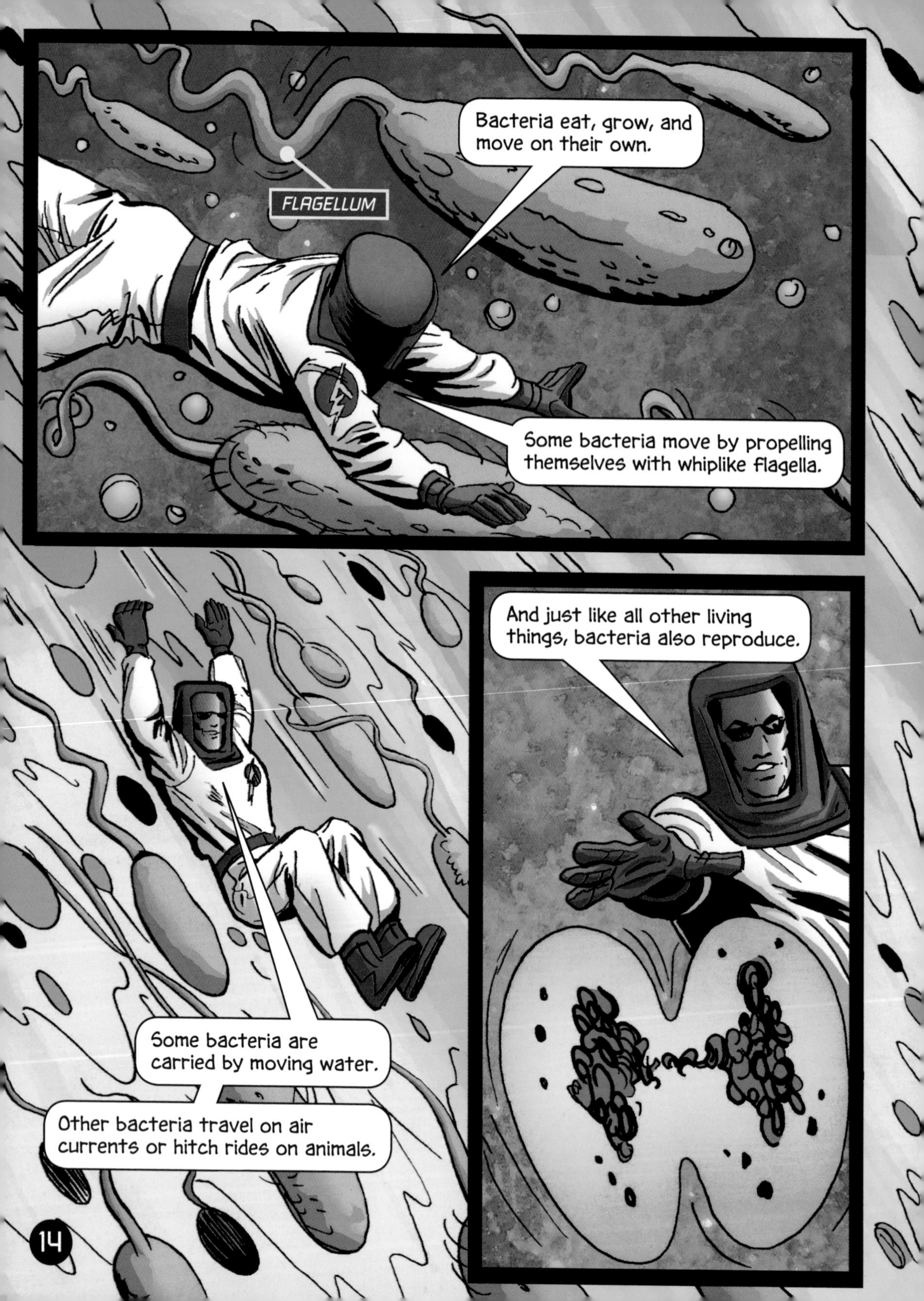
FLAGELLUM
Bacteria eat, grow, and move on their own.
Some bacteria move by propelling themselves with whiplike flagella.
Some bacteria are carried by moving water.
Other bacteria travel on air currents or hitch rides on animals.
And just like all other living things, bacteria also reproduce.

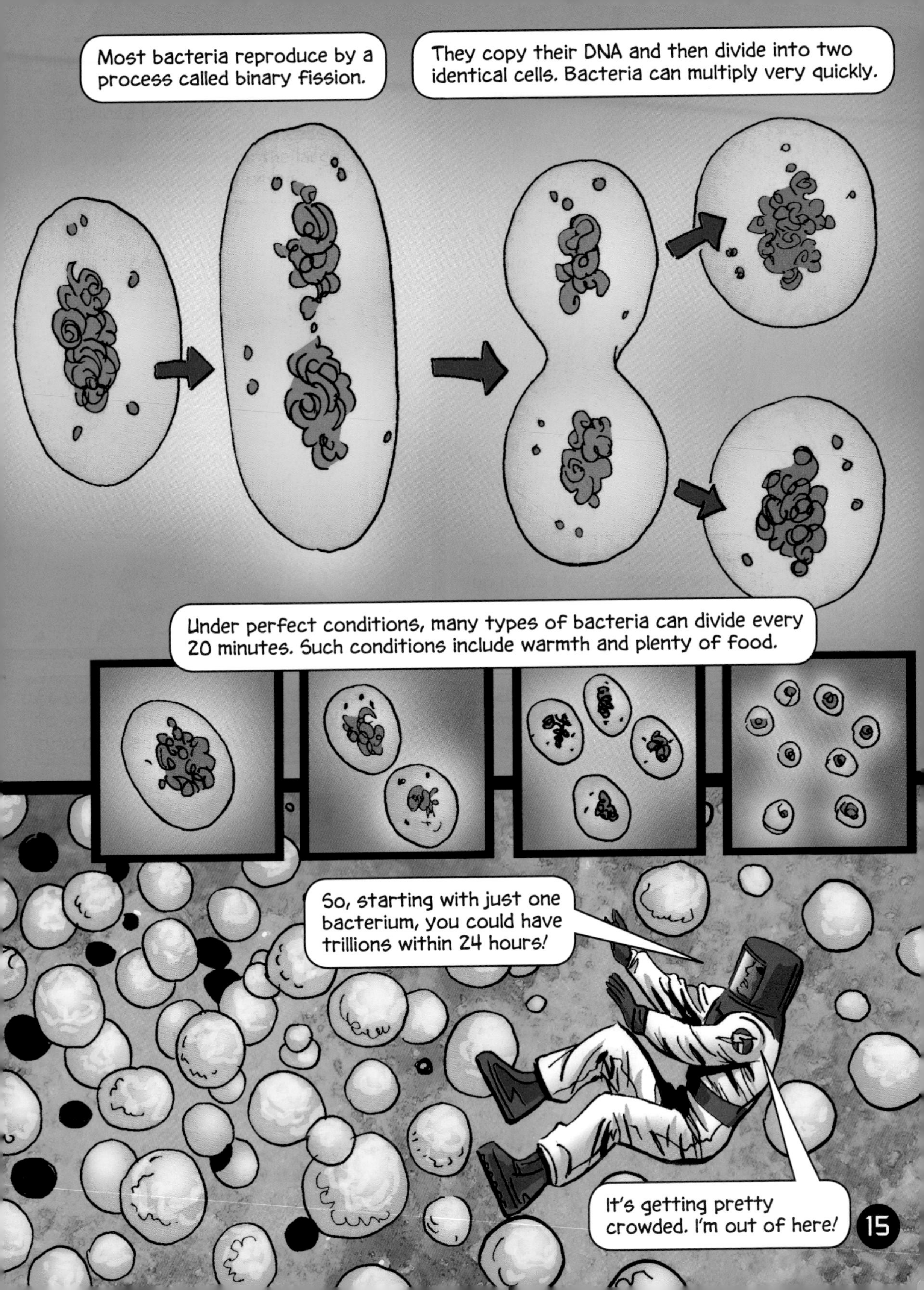
Most bacteria reproduce by a process called binary fission.
They copy their DNA and then divide into two identical cells. Bacteria can multiply very quickly.
Under perfect conditions, many types of bacteria can divide every 20 minutes. Such conditions include warmth and plenty of food.
So, starting with just one bacterium, you could have trillions within 24 hours!
It's getting pretty crowded. I'm out of here!

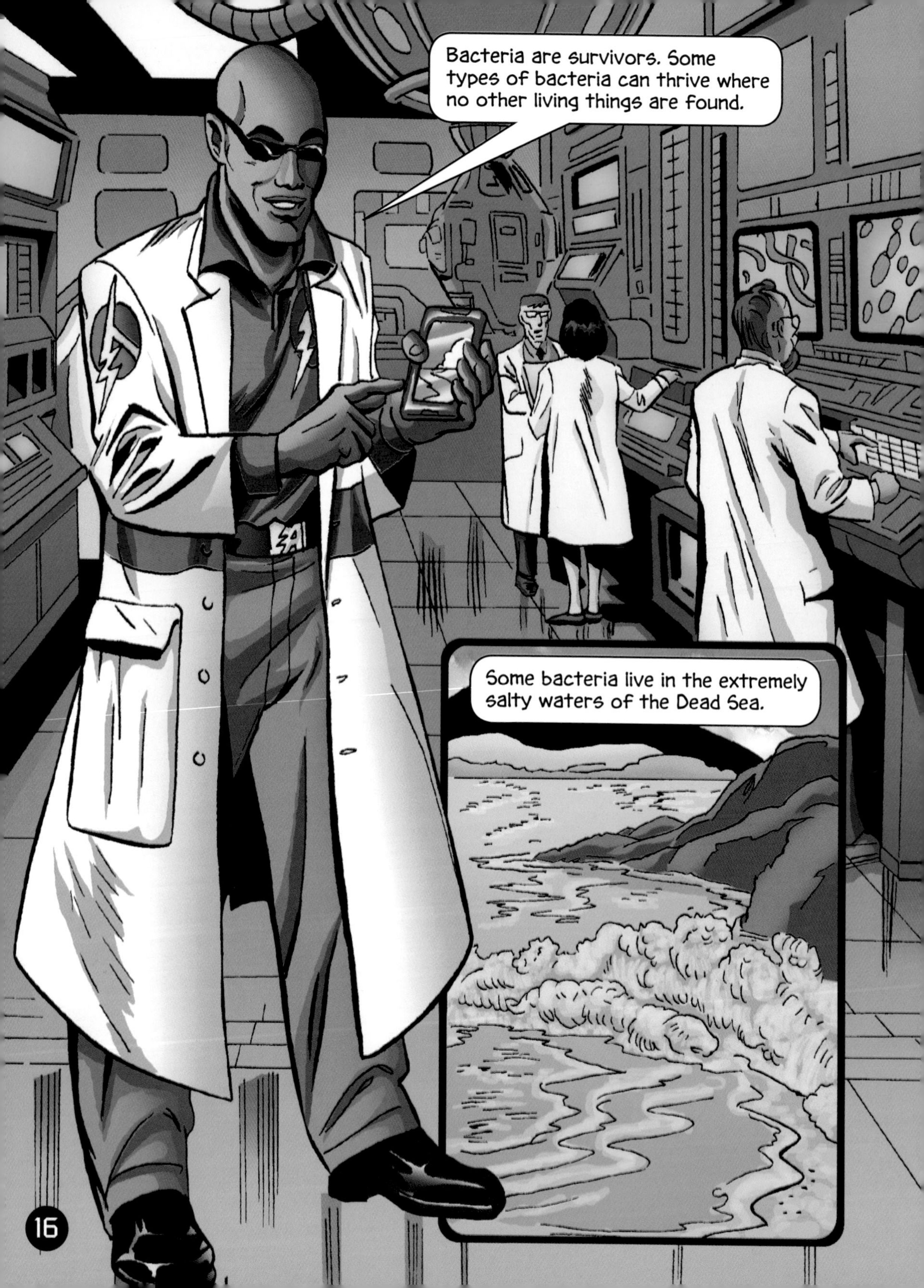
Bacteria are survivors. Some types of bacteria can thrive where no other living things are found.
Some bacteria live in the extremely salty waters of the Dead Sea.

Bacteria have been found deep under Antarctic ice.

They live in near-boiling temperatures at the hot springs of Yellowstone National Park.

Bacteria have even been found in clouds high above earth's surface.

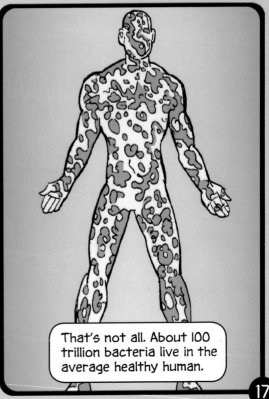

That's not all. About 100 trillion bacteria live in the average healthy human.

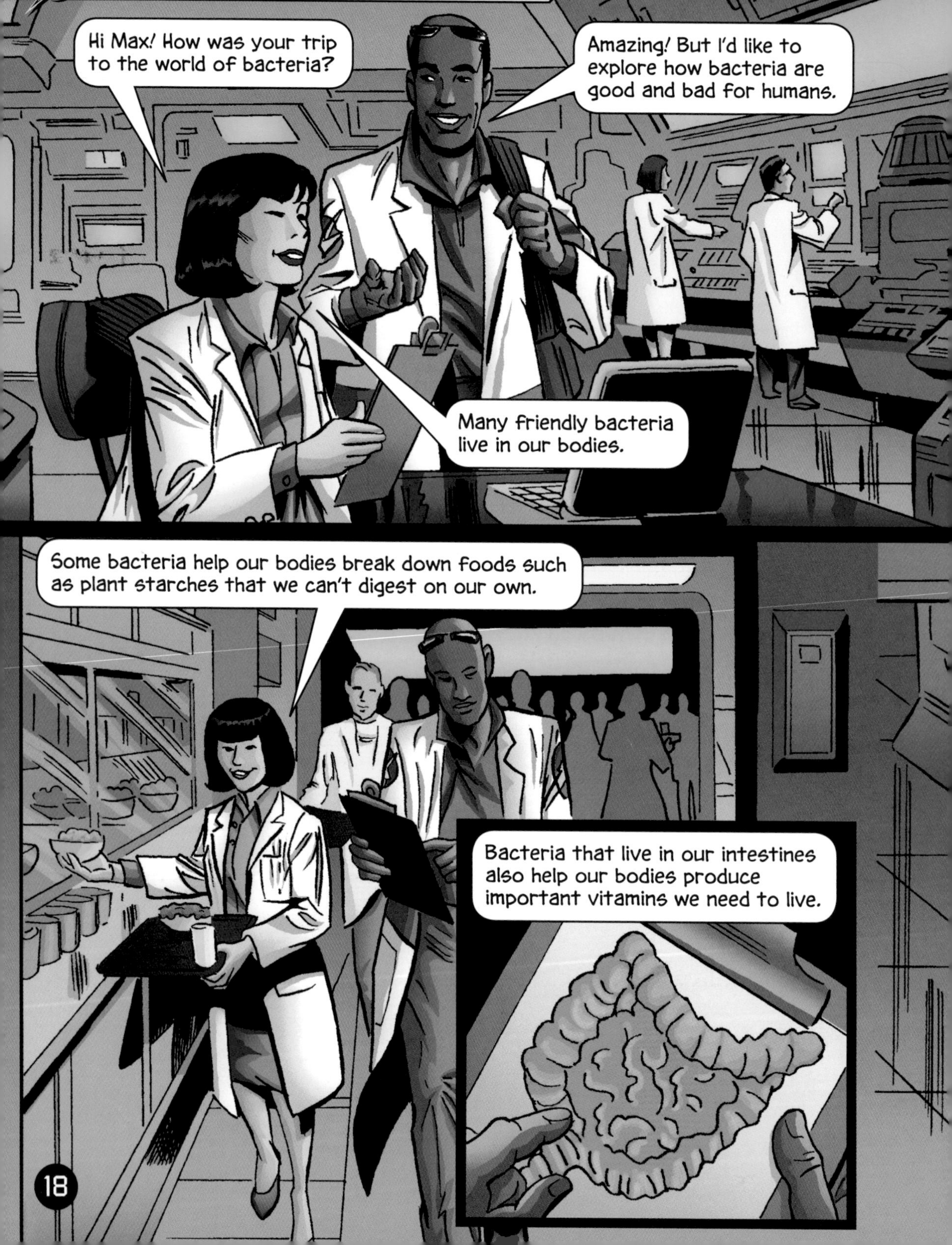
Hi Max! How was your trip to the world of bacteria?
Amazing! But I'd like to explore how bacteria are good and bad for humans.
Many friendly bacteria live in our bodies.
Some bacteria help our bodies break down foods such as plant starches that we can't digest on our own.
Bacteria that live in our intestines also help our bodies produce important vitamins we need to live.

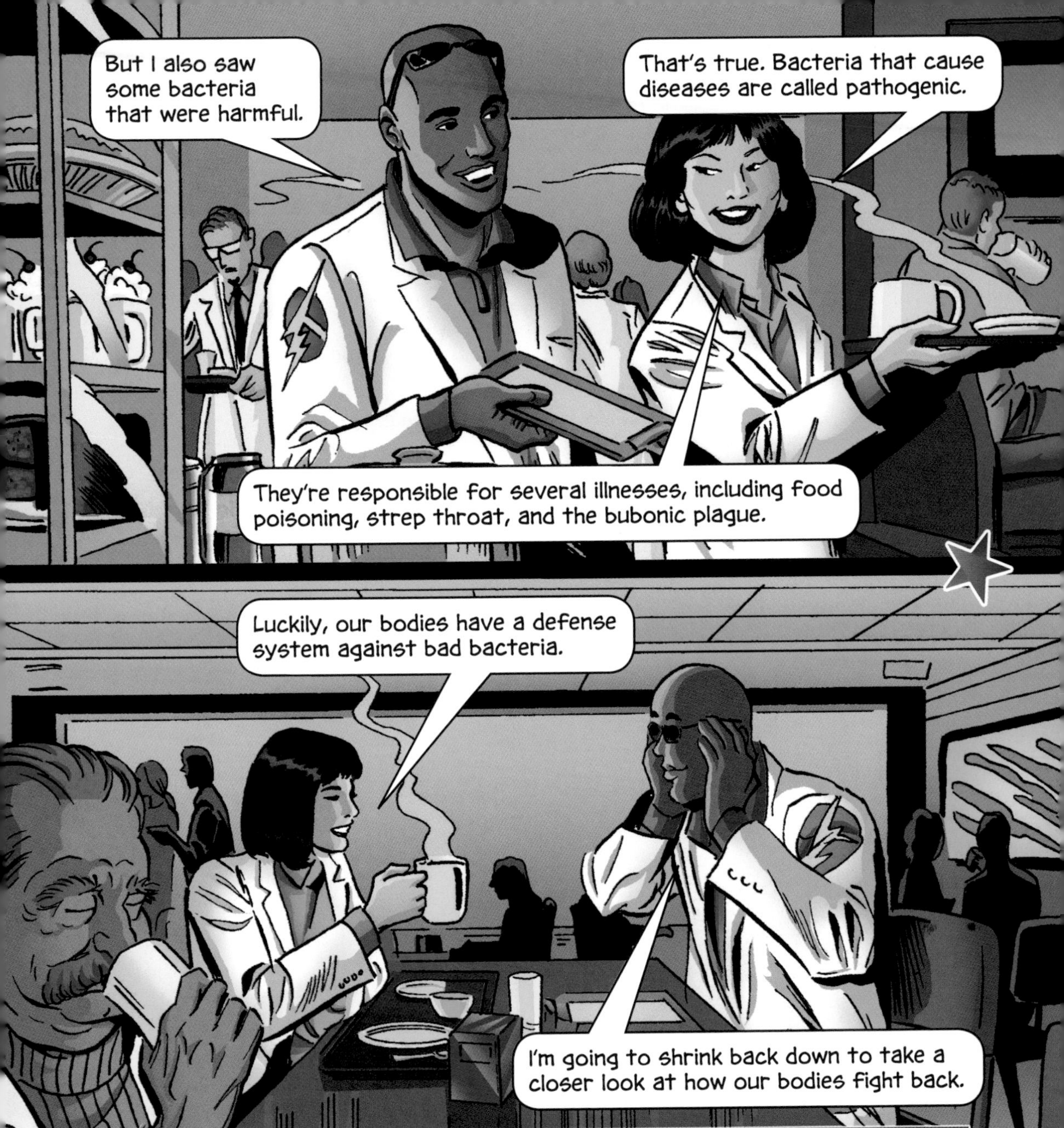
But I also saw some bacteria that were harmful.
That's true. Bacteria that cause diseases are called pathogenic.
They're responsible for several illnesses, including food poisoning, strep throat, and the bubonic plague.
Luckily, our bodies have a defense system against bad bacteria.
I'm going to shrink back down to take a closer look at how our bodies fight back.

BAD BACTERIA

ACCESS GRANTED: MAX AXIOM

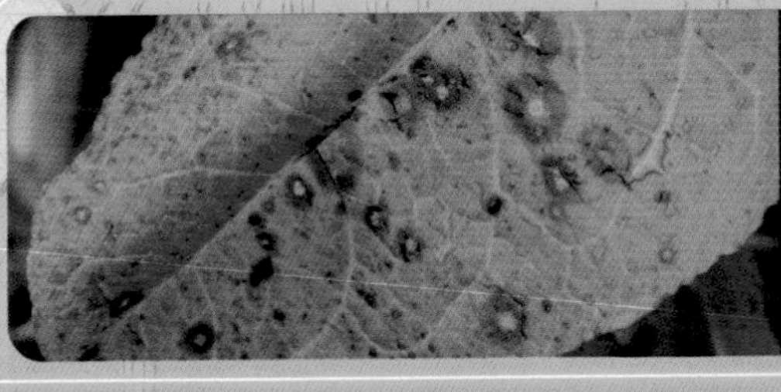

Pathogenic bacteria can attack plants, animals, fungi, and even other bacteria. Pathogenic bacteria can create holes in leaves by releasing toxins that damage cells.

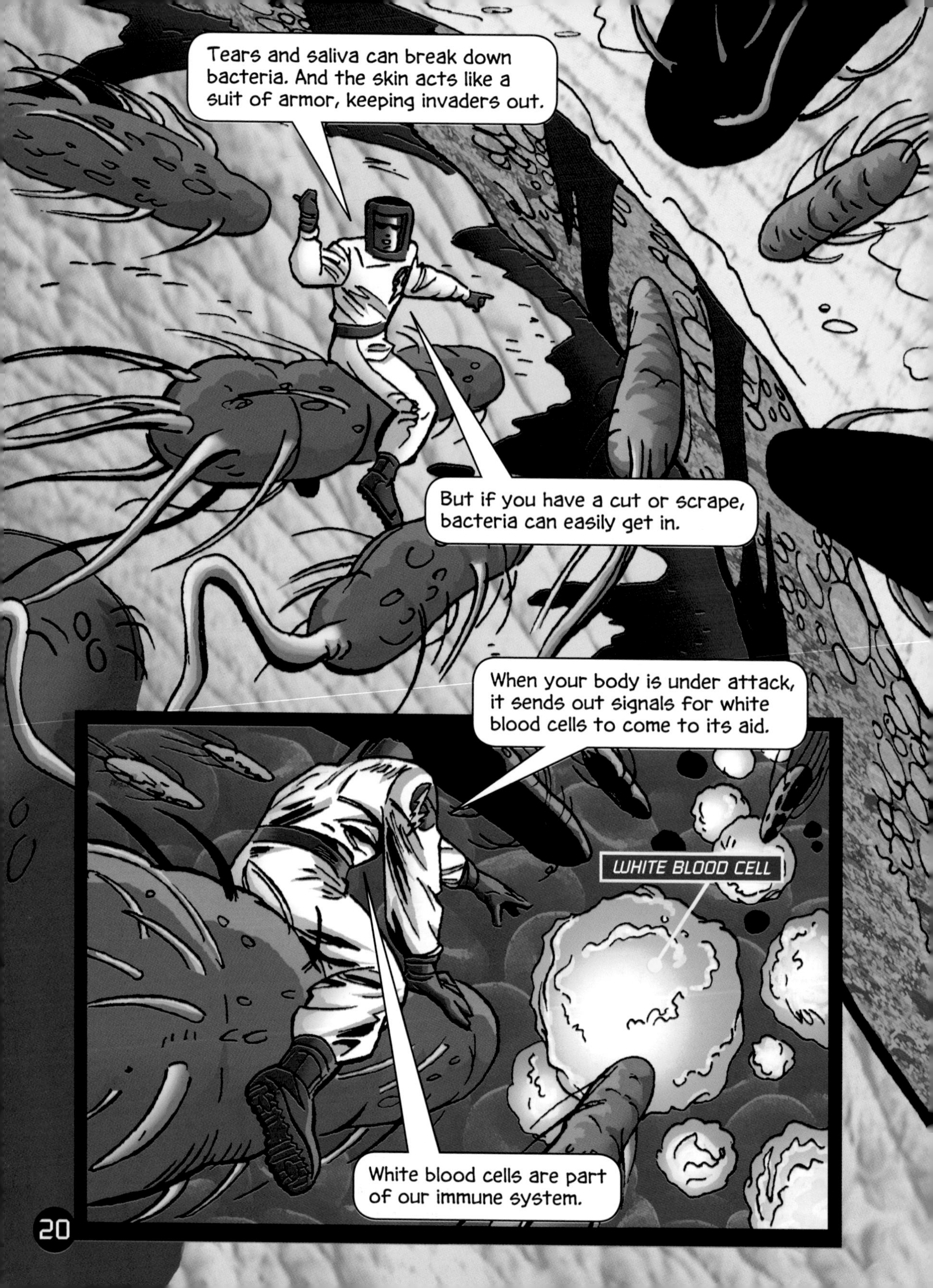
Tears and saliva can break down bacteria. And the skin acts like a suit of armor, keeping invaders out.
But if you have a cut or scrape, bacteria can easily get in.
When your body is under attack, it sends out signals for white blood cells to come to its aid.
WHITE BLOOD CELL
White blood cells are part of our immune system.

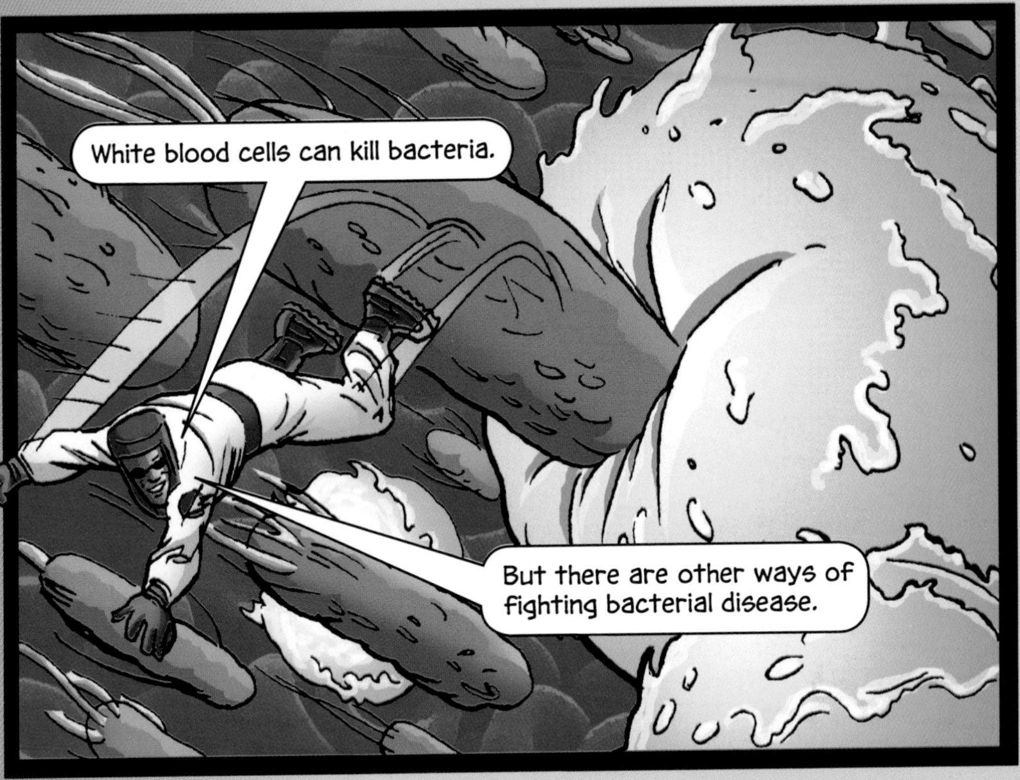
White blood cells can kill bacteria.
But there are other ways of fighting bacterial disease.

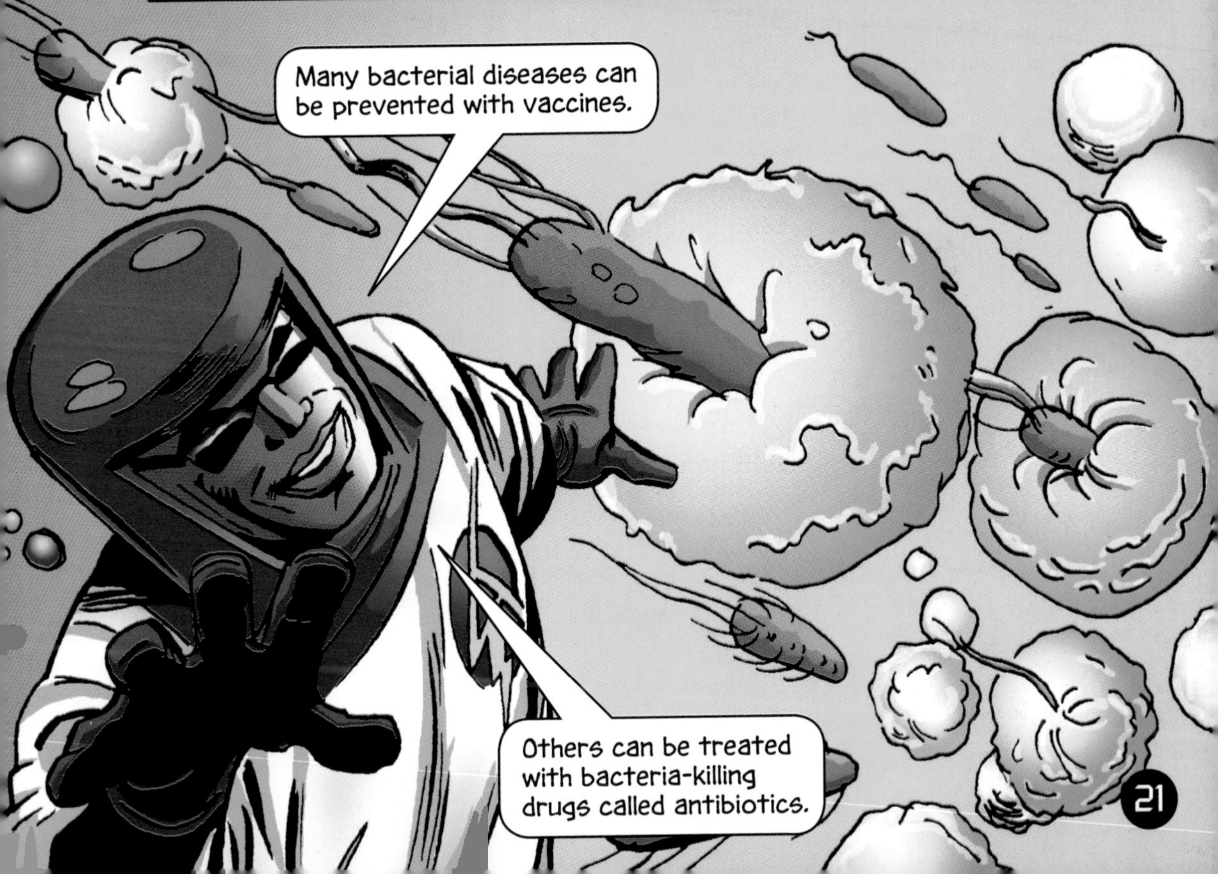
Many bacterial diseases can be prevented with vaccines.
Others can be treated with bacteria-killing drugs called antibiotics.

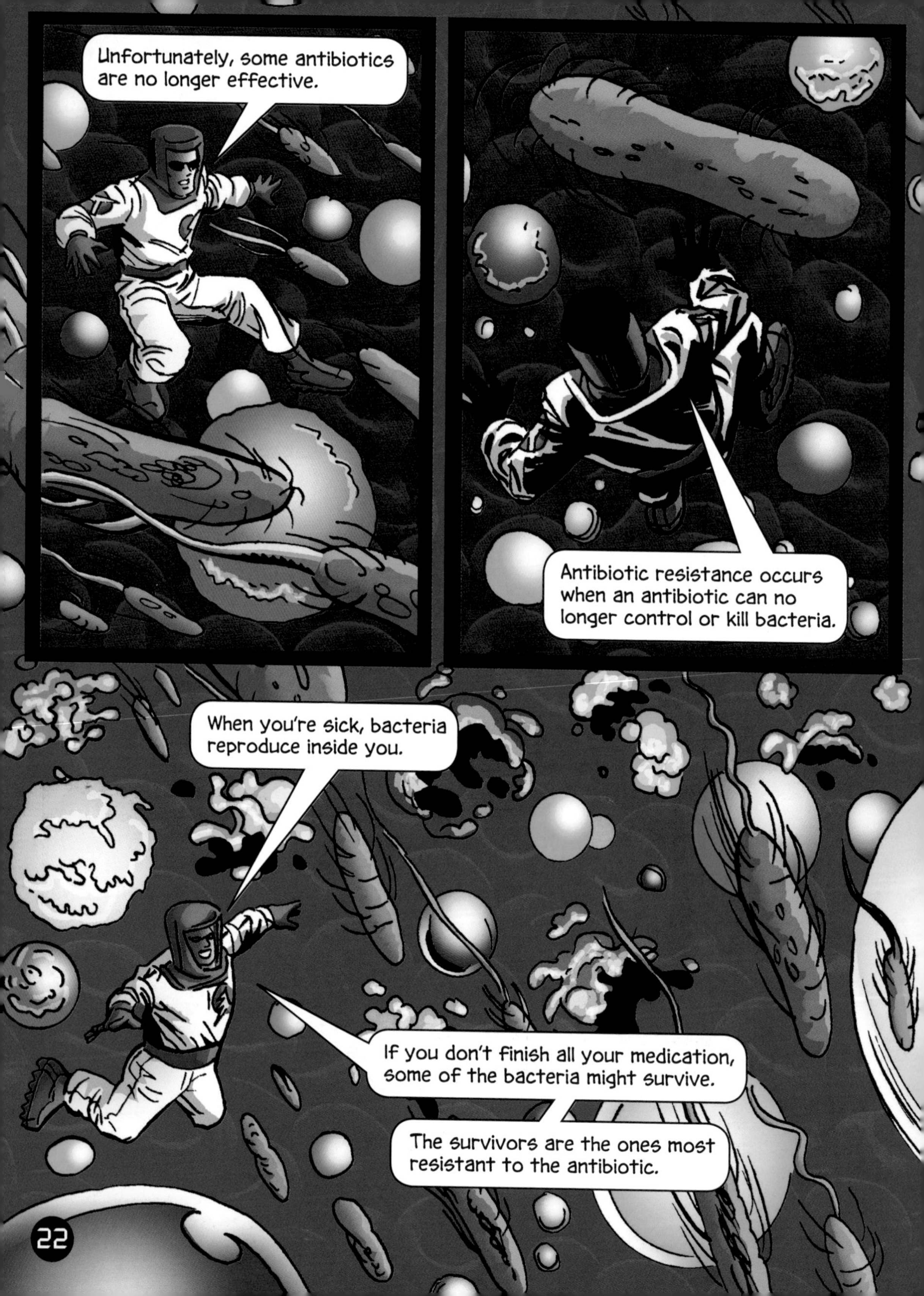
Unfortunately, some antibiotics are no longer effective.
Antibiotic resistance occurs when an antibiotic can no longer control or kill bacteria.
When you're sick, bacteria reproduce inside you.
If you don't finish all your medication, some of the bacteria might survive.
The survivors are the ones most resistant to the antibiotic.

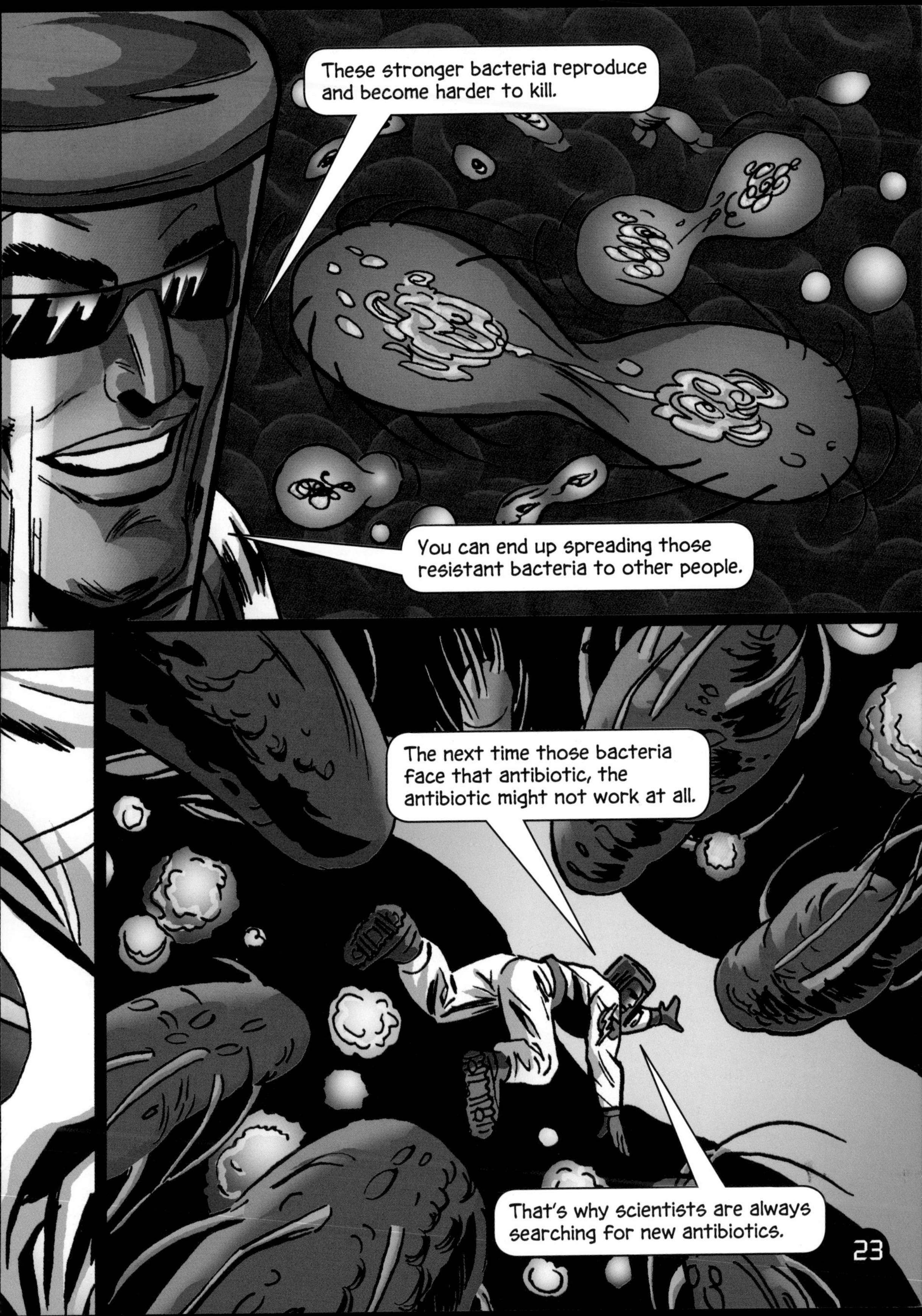
These stronger bacteria reproduce and become harder to kill.
You can end up spreading those resistant bacteria to other people.
The next time those bacteria face that antibiotic, the antibiotic might not work at all.
That's why scientists are always searching for new antibiotics.

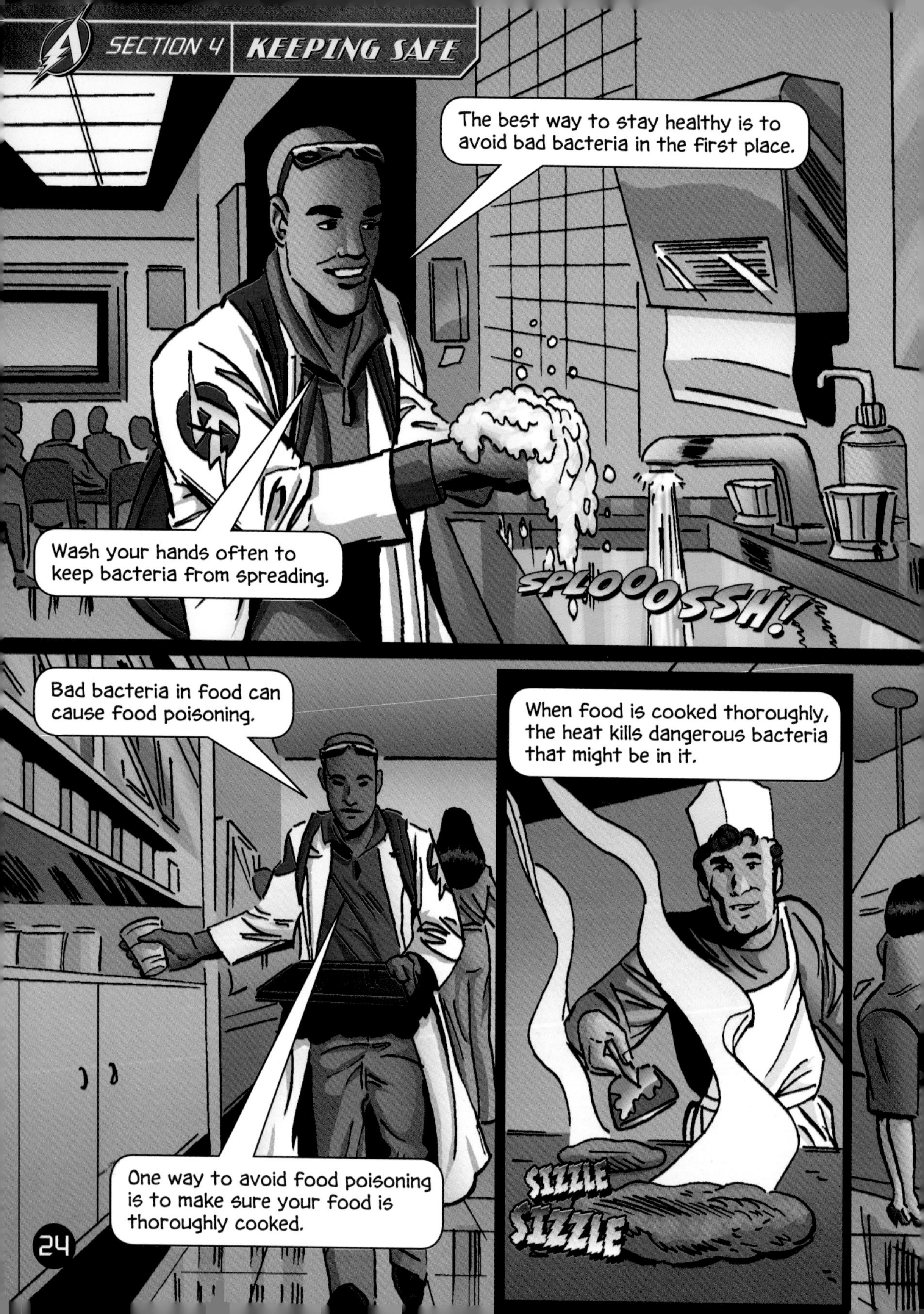
The best way to stay healthy is to avoid bad bacteria in the first place.
Wash your hands often to keep bacteria from spreading.
SPLOOOSSH!
Bad bacteria in food can cause food poisoning.
One way to avoid food poisoning is to make sure your food is thoroughly cooked.
When food is cooked thoroughly, the heat kills dangerous bacteria that might be in it.
SIZZLE
SIZZLE

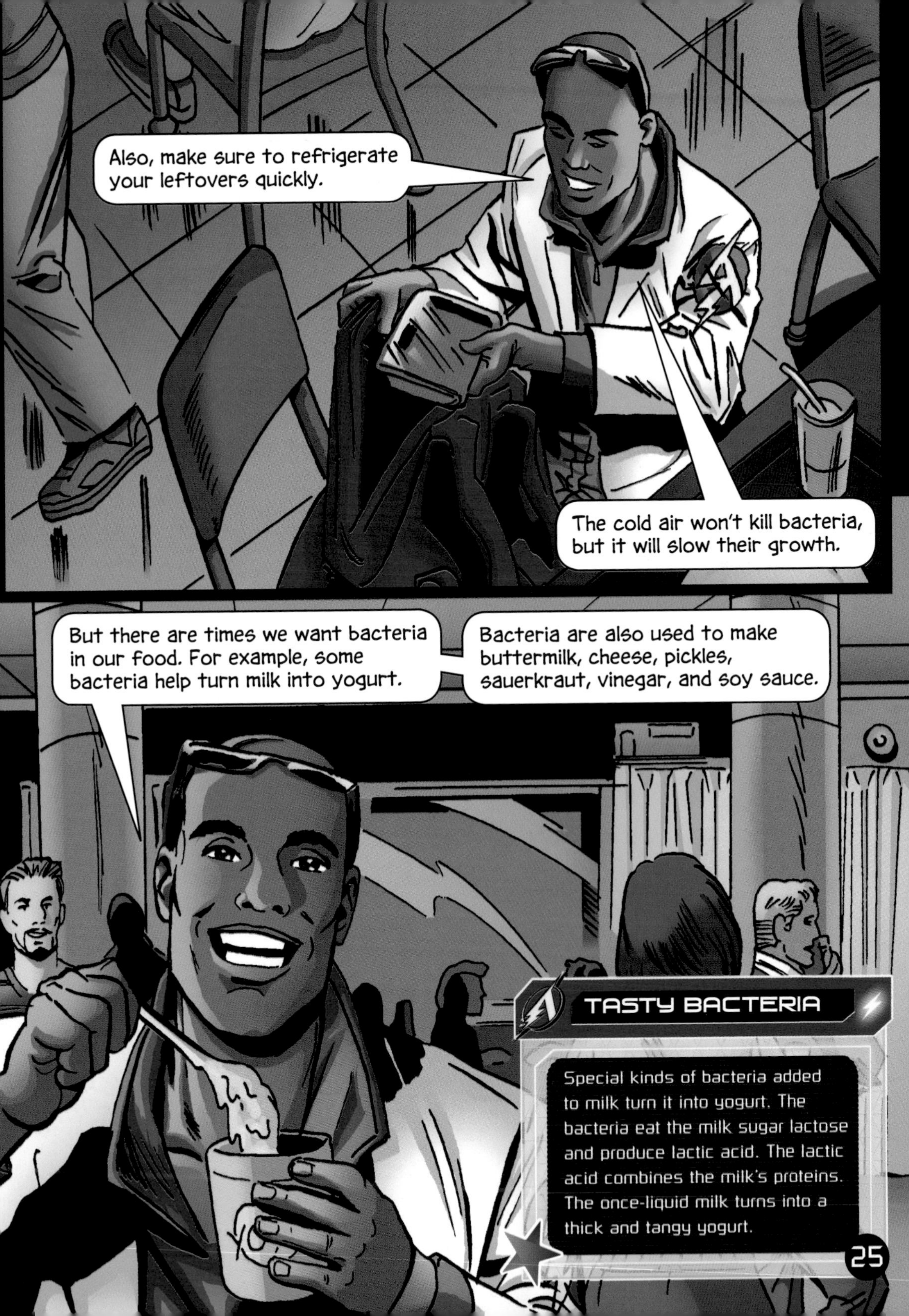
Also, make sure to refrigerate your leftovers quickly.
The cold air won't kill bacteria, but it will slow their growth.
But there are times we want bacteria in our food. For example, some bacteria help turn milk into yogurt.
Bacteria are also used to make buttermilk, cheese, pickles, sauerkraut, vinegar, and soy sauce.
TASTY BACTERIA
Special kinds of bacteria added to milk turn it into yogurt. The bacteria eat the milk sugar lactose and produce lactic acid. The lactic acid combines the milk's proteins. The once-liquid milk turns into a thick and tangy yogurt.

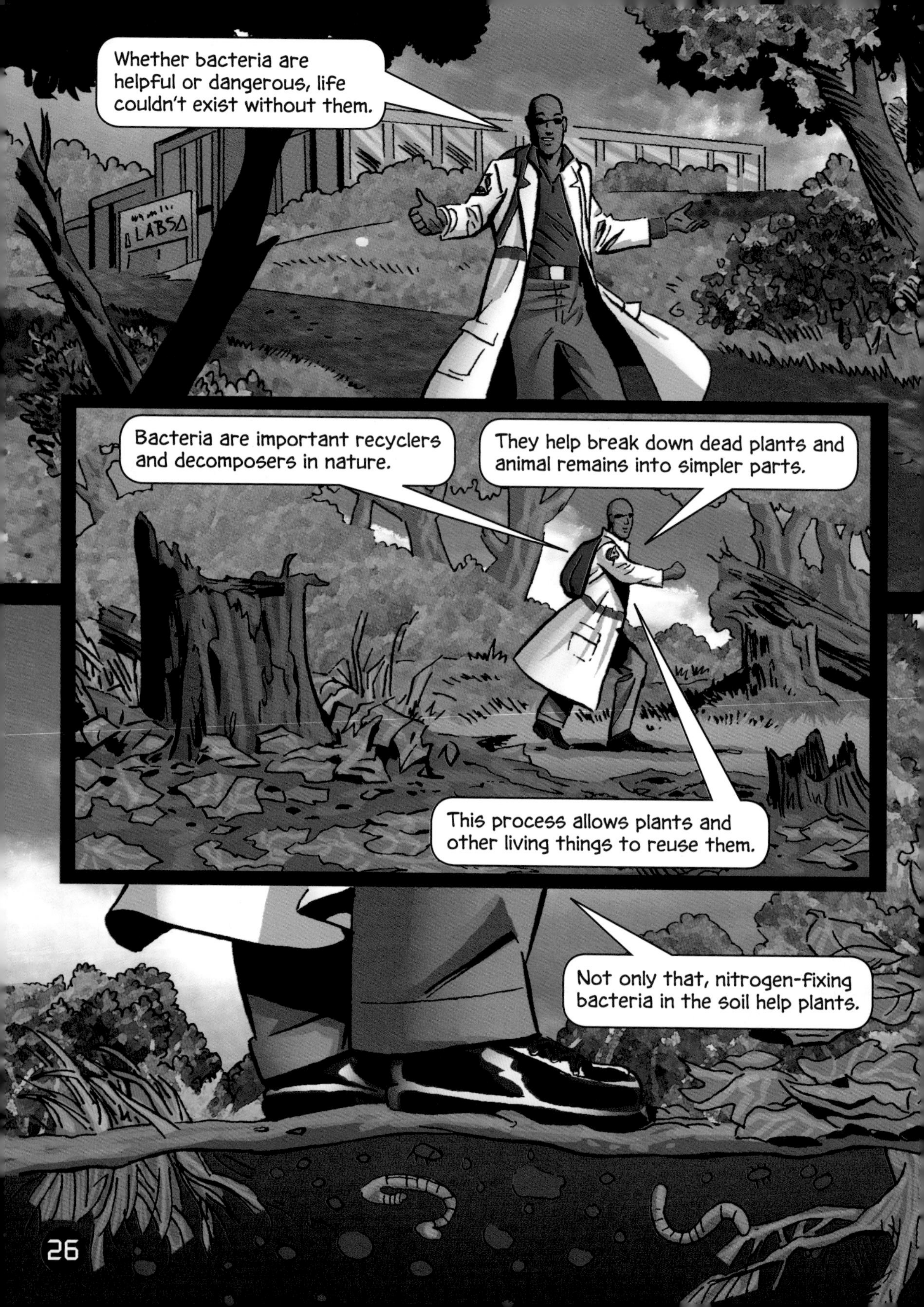
LABS
Whether bacteria are helpful or dangerous, life couldn't exist without them.
Bacteria are important recyclers and decomposers in nature.
They help break down dead plants and animal remains into simpler parts.
This process allows plants and other living things to reuse them.
Not only that, nitrogen-fixing bacteria in the soil help plants.

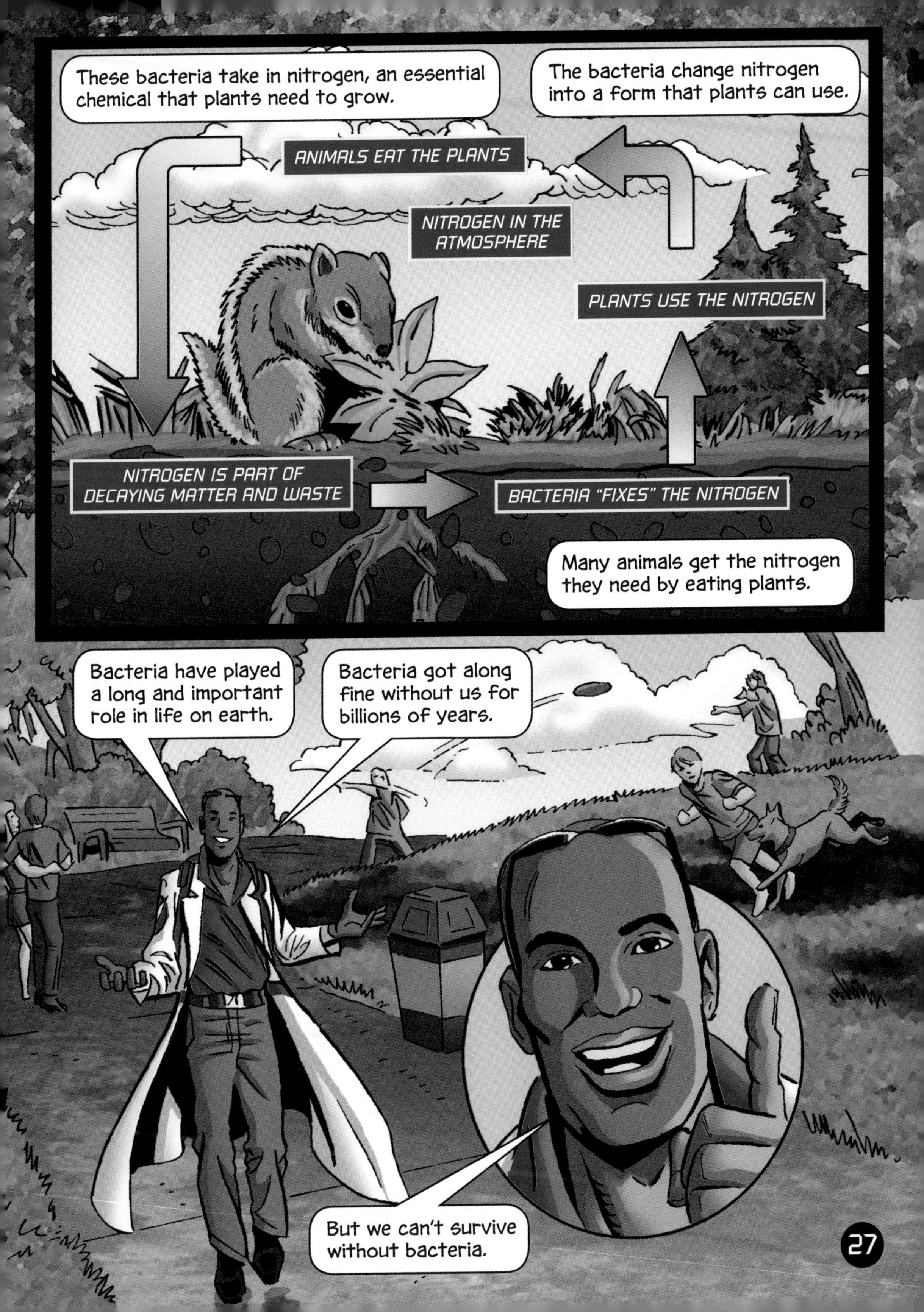
These bacteria take in nitrogen, an essential chemical that plants need to grow.
The bacteria change nitrogen into a form that plants can use.
ANIMALS EAT THE PLANTS
NITROGEN IN THE ATMOSPHERE
PLANTS USE THE NITROGEN
NITROGEN IS PART OF DECAYING MATTER AND WASTE
BACTERIA "FIXES" THE NITROGEN
Many animals get the nitrogen they need by eating plants.
Bacteria have played a long and important role in life on earth.
Bacteria got along fine without us for billions of years.
But we can't survive without bacteria.

Some giant bacteria are 1,000 times larger than normal bacteria. One, called *Epulopiscium fischelsoni*, is found in the intestines of surgeonfish. It's so big, it can be seen with the naked eye.

Anaerobic bacteria don't need oxygen to live. Anaerobic bacteria live in soil and even inside our bodies. They're mostly harmless. But if they travel to a part of the body where they don't belong, they can cause serious illness and disease.

In 1928, Alexander Fleming discovered that a type of common mold could kill pathogenic bacteria. He isolated the bacteria-killing chemical from the mold and called it penicillin. It was the first antibiotic ever discovered.

Bacteria that live in the stomachs of cows and other cud-chewing animals help them digest tough plants and grasses.

Botulinum toxin, a poison produced by *Clostridium botulinum* bacteria, is one of the most deadly naturally occurring substances known. Despite this fact, doctors use very small amounts of the toxin to treat some medical conditions. It is best known today for its use as Botox. It is injected into the face where it paralyzes muscles, helping reduce lines and wrinkles.

Vaccines have been made for bacterial diseases such as whooping cough, diphtheria, tetanus, and Lyme disease.

E. coli move by whipping their flagella. They can travel a distance equal to 25 times their length in only a second.

Bacteria have changed the face of the planet. About two or three billion years ago, bacteria that used sunlight for energy emerged. They also gave off oxygen in the process. Thanks to bacteria, the oxygen we depend on started appearing in earth's atmosphere.

BACTERIA BREAD

Bacteria is all around us, and a lot of it is just on your hands! With this experiment, see how mold forms with bacteria, and why it's important to wash your hands before eating!

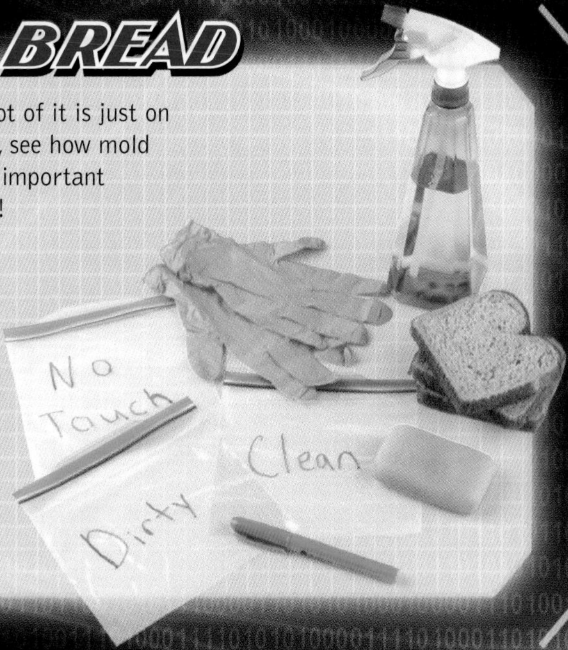

No Touch
Clean
Dirty

WHAT YOU NEED:

- permanent marker
- three zip-top sandwich bags
- disposable gloves
- 3 slices of wheat bread
- a spray bottle with water
- soap
- paper towel

WHAT YOU DO:

1. Use a marker to label the plastic bags. Label the first bag "not touched," the second bag "dirty hands," and the third bag "clean hands."
2. Put on the disposable gloves. Then pick up one piece of wheat bread and place it in the bag labeled "not touched."
3. Spray the bread twice with water and seal the bag.
4. Remove the disposable gloves. Touch nearby doorknobs, railings, or other surfaces in your house to add bacteria to your hands.
5. Pick up the second slice of bread with your bare hands. Gently touch the bread on all sides. Place the bread inside of the "dirty hands" bag. Spray the bread with water twice and seal the bag.
6. Thoroughly wash your hands with warm water and soap, and dry them with a paper towel.
7. Pick up the third slice of bread and touch on all sides with your bare hands. Place it in the bag labeled "clean hands." Spray the bread with water twice before sealing the bag.
8. Place the bags on a counter and observe the bags over the next six to seven days. Which slices of bread get mold on them? Do any grow mold more quickly?

DISCUSSION QUESTIONS

1. When are bacteria both helpful and harmful in our lives? Discuss some examples of each and form an argument defending why you think they are more helpful or harmful.

2. Antibiotics can be prescribed to treat diseases caused by bacteria. What are some downsides to antibiotics? What are some ways to avoid these downsides?

3. Would the world be a better place if all bacteria were killed? Discuss and explain your answer.

4. Bacteria play a big role in food poisoning. What can you do, in terms of cooking and refrigeration, to reduce the risk of food poisoning?

WRITING PROMPTS

1. In your own words, define bacteria. Then write a short paragraph explaining where they can be found.

2. Harmful bacteria can enter the body and cause diseases. Make a list of ways your body defends against the kinds of bacteria that can make you sick.

3. Some bacteria are helpful to plants. Write a short paragraph describing the ways bacteria can be useful to plants.

4. People did not know about bacteria until the late 1600s. Create a list of some reasons why they weren't discovered until then.

GLOSSARY

antibiotic (an-ti-bye-OT-ik)—a drug that kills bacteria and is used to cure infections and disease

bacilli (bah-SILL-ee)—rod-shaped bacteria

binary fission (BYE-ner-ee FI-shuhn)—form of reproduction where the DNA is copied and the bacteria splits into two cells

cell (SEL)—the smallest unit of a living thing

cocci (KAH-kye)—ball-shaped bacteria

decomposer (dee-kuhm-PO-zur)—a living thing that turns dead things into food for others

DNA (dee en AY)—the genetic material that carries all of the instructions to make a living thing and keep it working; DNA stands for deoxyribonucleic acid.

eukaryotic cell (u-kare-ee-AH-tik SEL)—a cell that has DNA enclosed in a nucleus

flagellum (flah-GEL-luhm)—a whiplike tail that helps bacteria move

immune system (i-MYOON SISS-tuhm)—the part of the body that protects against germs and diseases

microorganism (mye-kroh-OR-guh-niz-uhm)—a living thing too small to be seen without a microscope

prokaryotic cell (pro-kare-ee-AH-tik SEL)—a cell that does not have a nucleus

spirilla (spuh-RILL-ah)—spiral-shaped bacteria

vaccine (vak-SEEN)—dead or weakened germs injected into a person or animal to help fight disease

READ MORE

Baum, Margaux. *Bacteria*. Germs: Disease Causing Organisms Series. New York, NY: The Rosen Publishing Group, Incorporated, 2016.

Farndon, John. *Tiny Killers: When Bacteria and Viruses Attack*. Sickening History of Medicine Series. Minneapolis, MN: Lerner Publishing Group, 2017.

Gagne, Tammy. *Battling Against Drug-Resistant Bacteria*. North Mankato, MN: 12-Story Library, 2017.

Mould, Steve. *The Bacteria Book*. New York, NY: DK/Penguin Random House, 2018.

INTERNET SITES

Biology for Kids: Bacteria
https://www.ducksters.com/science/bacteria.php

Britannica Kids: Bacteria
https://kids.britannica.com/students/article/bacteria/273051

Biology4Kids
http://www.biology4kids.com/files/micro_bacteria.html

Super-cool stuff! Check out projects, games, and lots more at
www.capstonekids.com

INDEX